He
Speaks

By: Sonya J.
Smith

Limits of Liability and Disclaimer of Warranty

The author and publisher shall not be liable for your misuse of this material. This book is a fictional work and created strictly for informational and educational purposes.

Warning – Disclaimer

The purpose of this book is to educate and entertain. The author and/or publisher shall have neither liability nor responsibility to anyone concerning any loss or damage caused, or alleged to be caused, directly or indirectly by the information contained in this book.

Table of Contents

---

*My sheep listen to my
voice, I know them, and
they follow me.*

John 10:27 NIV

Dedication:

I am dedicating this book to my parents Al and Beverly Jones. Proverbs 22:6, *"Train up a child in the way he should go and when he is old, he will not depart from it."* I want you both to know that I am truly blessed to have you as my parents. You are gifts to me. Each day I watched you exemplify what it meant to live for God making no apologies. All my life, you have been saved! Thank you for loving me unconditionally and loving my husband as if he was your own son. Loving and spoiling my children. My prayer is that as you read this book, it lets you know that everything you instilled in me was not in vain. The Word was inside of me, and it did not depart.

Acknowledgments:

I would like to first acknowledge and thank my Heavenly Father! You have never left me. You've kept me many dark days and nights. It's because of you that I live and breathe! I thank You for Your grace, Your Mercy, Your Peace, and Your love for me. Lord, thank You for not giving up on me. There are no words in the English language that can express how grateful I am to You. I honor You and I love You.

My husband Derek, my high school sweetheart, we have literally grown up together. I have shared some of the most amazing moments of my life with you and some of the darkest. Our journey has not been easy, but we are still standing. I often reflect on the prayer that was prayed over our union and I ask God to honor it. Thank you for loving me.

My children: Jay'lah, D.J. and Dai'ya, the three of you are my heartbeats! I love you more than life itself. You challenge me to be a great mom. As much as I try to teach and protect you, I also have learned from each of you. Mommy loves you so much.

My sister Faye, thank you for pushing me. Thank you for helping me to see myself how God sees me. Thank you for encouraging me to write this book. You have been my cheerleader, even when I didn't want to cheer myself on. You help to hold me accountable. I love you dearly and I am blessed to have you in my life.

Princess, thank you for listening as I read many of my writings to you. Thank you for being a listening ear and keeping me encouraged throughout this process.

Pastor Jackie, Momma Cynthia, Permission Room thank you! Pastor Jackie if it weren't for the Permission Room, I truly believe I would still be stuck. Thank you for your obedience to God. Your yes has helped to free so many women. Momma Cynthia Ware you are a gem for the Kingdom!

Tamika Sims thank you for guiding me through this process.

To my entire village that has been with me over the years through all of my ups and downs I say thank you, to those of you who have prayed with me and for me, thank you. Ma Katie, Pastor Ren, Tammy, Kembley, Patrice, and all of my sisters, too many to name, you know who you are. I love you all so much!

I pray God's blessings over each of you.
You all have blessed my life.

Introduction:

My dear friend, thank you for choosing this book at this moment. I believe it is not a coincidence, it was ordained by God. I have prayed for every reader. This is a collection of years of writings that I was encouraged to share with others. I am so glad I did. I hope that through reading the pages that follow, you are encouraged to open your heart and begin to have open and honest dialogue with our Heavenly Father. My prayer is that you will no longer put God in a box because He is too grand to be boxed in. I want you to know that *He Speaks!* You must first believe that He speaks. Believe me. He longs to have conversations with us.

Some of these passages came at moments in my life when I felt so alone. If anyone looked at me from the outside, then you would think that I had it altogether. However, the battle and war I was fighting internally nearly took me out. One day while at work, sitting at my desk, face turned away from others so they could not see the tears falling down my face, I encountered my Savior. I was praying to God. I needed Him so desperately. Suddenly, a voice said to me, *"Open your drawer. Look under those papers and get that CD out of that case."* "Am I crazy?" I asked myself, but I knew I needed to listen to that voice! I followed every instruction. I placed the CD on my computer, the first song played was not the song! The song I was led to was *"Will you trust me?"* by Donnie McClurkin

Proverbs 3:5-6 KJV, *"Trust in the Lord with all thine heart; and lean not unto thine own understanding. In all thy ways acknowledge him, and he shall direct thy paths."*

As I listened to every word of that song, the tears flowed even more as I knew that God was speaking to me. I prayed to the Lord, *please, don't let anyone come to my desk.* When the song was over, I felt a pressing to write, and I haven't stopped. I can be sitting, and the urge will hit me. I'll have to stop what I am doing and write. He speaks! The wonderful thing about our Father is that He doesn't speak in only one way. He speaks through His Word. He speaks through song. He speaks through other people. He speaks through the wind, the birds. He will speak through Creation. He speaks through worship and prayer!

These are just a few ways that our Father speaks. If you really want to hear Him speak, then I dare you to develop an intimate relationship with God. He wants you to sit in His Presence opening your heart, body , and soul to Him. He says in His Word, *"If you draw near to me, then I will draw near to you."*

James 4:8 KJV, "Draw nigh to God, and he will draw nigh to you. Cleanse your hands, ye sinners; and purify your hearts, ye double minded."

God is so funny. As I was writing, that's the Scripture He led me to. Oh, how I love Him! He amazes me!

I feel the need to tell you that God speaking to you doesn't exempt you from going through life's struggles. However, because

He speaks you are guaranteed that He will give you instructions. The truth of the matter is, He is waiting for you to talk it over with Him. For He is the God that will give you peace in the middle of every storm.

Psalms 107: 28-31 KJV , "Then they cry unto the Lord in their trouble, and he bringeth them out of their distresses. He maketh the storm calm, so that the waves thereof are still. Then they are glad because they be quiet, so he bringeth them to their desired haven. Oh, that men would praise the Lord for his goodness, and for his wonderful works to the children of men!"

Nahum 1:7 KJV, *"The Lord is good, a strong hold in the day of trouble; and he knoweth them that trust in him."*

Isaiah 25:4-5 KJV, "For thou hast been a strength to the poor, a strength to the needy in his distress, a refuge from the storm, a shadow from the heat, when the blast of the terrible one is a storm against the wall. Thou shalt bring down the noise of strangers, as the heat in a dry place; even the heat with

the shadow of a cloud; the branch of the
terrible ones shall be brought low."

These are only a few Scriptures to encourage you.

Trust me. God cares about whatever concerns you so there is nothing too small or too big for Him. He wants to hear about it all.

1 Peter 5:7, *"Casting all your care upon him; for he careth for you."*

I hope by the end of this book if you haven't already started, you will begin to have conversations with God, expecting to hear from Him. If you've stopped talking to God, I encourage you to start back. He is waiting to hear from you again. If that means Lord, I won't move until I hear from you then that's exactly what you say. Let me ask you: How *desperate are you to hear from Him?*

Hearing from Him takes repetition. I also hope that many of these passages encourage you. If you've felt that you were alone, I pray by the end of this book, you realize that you are not. Pick up a notebook and a pen. Sit. Ask God to send you to a Scripture, walk in a bookstore. Ask Him to lead you to a book. Lord, what song will you have me listen to today? Or a simple, *Good morning, Jesus*. I invite you to hear, listen, and even feel His presence because simply put, He Speaks!

Who Am I?

"I will praise thee; for I am fearfully and wonderfully made; marvelous are thou, thy works; and that my soul knoweth right well."

Psalm 139:14 KJV

Who am I? I often ask myself as I look in the mirror at this brown round face. Who am I? As I sit and pray and think. Who am I? As I talk, as I look and as I hear others seemingly sure about their choices, their path in life. Then I ask, why don't I know who I am? Why am I confused about where I should be? Why do I not know what I was created to be. Why do I feel like I have failed? Have I wasted precious energy? Have I taken the wrong path towards my destiny! I thought I'd be a counselor, helping others make a difference, not just a wife, a mother, and a professional. Who am I?

Then one day the thought came to me. Did I ever ask the One that designed me? Did I ask Him what He created me to be? Did I ask Him His will for me? As children, we are asked what do you want to be when you grow up? I had an answer then, maybe a princess when I was three, a nurse when I was 10, an English teacher when I was 14 and then fear sat in. A counselor by the time I was 17, and then I started towards that journey when college began. I will not go into my life story but a mother, a wife, a daughter, a sister, a friend. Those are some of my accomplishments and I have not always been the best at each of them. Who am I?

When I found Christ, I realized who I am. God's child, brown round face, renewed mother, wife, sister, daughter, and friend. When I struggle with those accomplishments, I kneel and pray to Him. My prayers also changed to Lord I want to be who You created me to be! I want to fulfill every plan You have for me. You see to Him; I am not only those things. He has shown me that not only do I touch their lives, but I bring inspiration and happiness to many that are not a part of my immediate circle. I offer a kind word, a bright smile, and grace. I am learning to exemplify the woman of God He's destined me to be. I've also prayed for Him to help me see the me that He sees. And not only see the me that he sees but become the me He has destined for me to be. This isn't where my story ends, but where the journey begins for every aspect of my life, I place it in His hands.

Listen & Obey: What is God Speaking to You

1.   How does God see you?

_____

_____

2.   How do you see yourself?

_____

_____

The Gift

"For God so loved the world, that he gave his only begotten son, that whosoever believeth in him should not perish, but have everlasting life."

John 3:16 KJV

God gave us a gift. It did not come wrapped in a box with beautiful paper and ribbon. The gift was delivered through a woman like me. She was a virgin! As the gift was delivered, I imagined her eyes were bright, the smile on her face and the love in her heart was like mine and yours when we pulled back the paper and removed the ribbon, wondering what was inside. Unlike me, she knew the gift that she was to receive. The best gift this world would ever have. No stipulations, no cost, it would be free. That gift was and is the Son of God. The difference? Her gift was a gift to all who would and is willing to accept it. Not wrapped in pretty paper with a bow to be untied. Her gift that was to be delivered through her from God eventually paid the ultimate sacrifice. The gift would sacrifice His own life for us. He would be lied on, cursed, wounded, and eventually die.

All these things He already knew but still He walked, taught, preached, and worked miracle after miracle. He would be nailed, stoned, bleed, cry out to His Father, *"Lord why hast thou forsaken me?"* The gift would die! Many would mourn. Others would rejoice as His body was stretched out on the cross, nails in His hands, head eventually hung low. Lifeless, He would appear! I would imagine many walked away not knowing what really occurred. Three days later the gift would rise from the dead. The tomb where He laid, He would not be there.

The gift God gave was His only begotten Son through the virgin Mary, a human! Spirit, Man, Lord and Savior in one to be accepted by all. The greatest gift ever given to man.

Listen & Obey: What is God Speaking to You

1.   How does the life you live show appreciation to what Jesus did for you?

_____

_____

2.   What did it cost Jesus to ensure our freedom?

_____

_____

12/30/2010

Lord, I look to You for help. The joy and peace that You give me in the midst of adversity is so amazing. I can smile and laugh in the storm because you remind me of Your promises. I know that there is hope for tomorrow. It's in the midnight hour when all seems to be lost that you lift me up out of the darkness. I must continue to travel on the road to righteousness for it is the only way.

The Word says that only the righteous will one day see His face. I must rest upon His Word. If I obey Him, keep His commandments, seek Him, and praise Him then I shall not worry or fear. I know without a shadow of doubt that He will take care of me and supply all of my needs. I am His child and His promise to me, He'll keep.

Listen & Obey: What is God Speaking to You

1. What is it that you need to give to God so that you can have peace?

_____

_____

2. What are the changes you need to make so that you can be in right standing with God?

_____

_____

3. How will you allow God in so that He can help transform your life daily?

_____

_____

A God of Provision

"Consider the ravens: They do not sow or reap; they have no storeroom or barn; yet God feeds them. And how much more valuable you are than birds!"

Luke 12:24 NIV

You'll give me what I need when I need it most. I thought and still think I know what I need. The truth is God knows exactly what I need and when I need it most. It can be frustrating, as you sit and reflect over all the things in your life that seem to be going wrong. You begin to get angry and confused. Lord, I've come to you over and over again with the same issues, the same hurts, the same sickness, I've asked you over and over for deliverance, for a breakthrough, but nothing Lord nothing! What am I today? I'm tired, weary, and worn! I am ready to give up! I am doubting you. I've been in this place for so long, Lord. I look around and I see people who could care less about living for

You. I see them prosper. While I, Your child, have come before You over and over and still nothing has changed. Nothing has changed! My family is still being torn apart, my finances are still a mess, my friends have left me, and my child has turned his back on me. My husband is running to and fro. My Life is in shambles. I have sought You and still nothing! Are you there, Lord, are You listening? Why hast thou forsaken me? Why have you left me here to struggle alone? Lord, I give up!

Then He asks why do you not trust me? Why have you not sat still and listened to me? Why have you not kept the faith? Why have you not continued to praise me? Why are you looking at this as if you are defeated? Ask yourself, have you truly done all that is required of you? Trust me when things are good and bad? Believe in me when it seems like I have left you? When you bring your burdens to me, leave them with me? They are mine not yours. Remember everything is not as it seems. I've heard all your cries. I know all your concerns. While you are wallowing in self-pity, have I not kept you?

Have I not fed you? Even in the worst of times my grace is sufficient. Did I not say to Cast your cares on me because I care for you? I'll never leave you! I'll never forsake you! I am the true and living God! I'm here! Your prayers have been answered and the doors are being opened. I always keep my word. Trust in me! I am the only way. I'll see you through and bless you abundantly. Always remember that "All things, not some things work together for the good of those that love me! You will be blessed in my time not yours because I know what is best.

I know you are hurting. I know you're doubting me. I know the burdens that you carry and answers that you seek. It seems that I have left you in this world alone. It's by your side I've been protecting you all along. You may not see it now, or understand the trials that you face, know that I'm here to help you win this race. Just count on me to see you through. Give it all to me as I know what's best for you. When you give it to me don't look back, trust in my words and don't get off track. When you begin to doubt just begin to pray and fall on your knees and I will sway you, my way.

I'm always the answer, there is no other way. I'll bring out the sun to brighten up your day. Draw close to me and I'll draw near to you. Let me be your Savior as God created me to.

Listen & Obey: What is God Speaking to You

1. Can you think of a season or time in your life that you felt that God was not hearing your prayers? Describe that season.

_____

_____

2. They say hindsight is 20/20 vision, describe how God showed up and showed out?

_____

_____

Dream Again

"Trust in the Lord with all thine heart; and lean not unto thine own understanding. In all thy ways acknowledge him, and he shall direct thy paths."

Proverbs 3:5-6

God says dream again! We tend to lose focus as life happens to us. We put our dreams on the shelf or we stop believing in ourselves because life has brought us so many twists and turns. God says to dream again! When we were children, we acted out our dreams. We played with our friends and loved ones acting out the part of the thing we saw ourselves being. Placing ourselves in the places we wanted to visit. God says to dream again! Have childlike excitement! Have childlike faith! This time bringing those dreams to the Father, acting out the part, preparing yourself for that thing to become reality because this time we are walking by faith not by sight.

Trusting and knowing with God all things are possible. If it is in His will, it shall come to pass. If He promised it, you shall see it. Believe like you did as a child with such excitement knowing that it shall come to pass. Do the work. Wear the clothes. Walk in it as if it has already come to pass. Do not waiver. Dream again! It's a command from your daddy!

Listen & Obey: What is God Speaking to You

1.   What dreams have you put on the shelf or have forgotten about?

_____

_____

2.   Write out a prayer to God concerning those dreams.

_____

_____

Find Rest In Me

"Come unto me, all ye that labour and are heavy laden, and I will give you rest. Take my yoke upon you, and learn of me, for I am meek and lowly in heart; and ye shall find rest unto your souls. For my yoke is easy, and my burden is light."

Matthew 11:28-30 KJV

Find rest in me. As you go about your life, find rest in me. When your heart is heavy, and the burdens of this world begin to weigh you down, find rest in me. Stop carrying the weight not only alone, but I command that you stop carrying it and release it to me so that I can give you rest. In my arms, there is peace in the middle of the storm. In my arms, there is grace to carry you through the storm. In my arms, you will find rest. Rest like no other resting place. The safest place for you to be is in the arms of the Almighty God!

My arms are large enough and wide enough to hold not only you, but everything that is concerning you. I will take each one of your concerns and perfect them one-by-one, all while teaching you. All while showing you the areas of your life that I want to help you change so that rest in me comes naturally. It is my desire to fill you with My presence so that you know without a shadow of doubt that all that troubles you, troubles Me! In that assurance you know that I will not put more on you than you can bare. Strengthening confidence in knowing that I will always show up, so you need not worry, but rest.

Listen & Obey: What is God Speaking to You

1.   When you are facing difficulties in life, who is the first person you turn to?

_____

_____

2.   How does trusting God show up in your life during difficult times? How does that look for you?

_____

_____

3/12/21

My desire and where I place my eyes at, is the heart. I am looking for a pure heart. A pure willing heart. A heart that truly wants to serve me. The heart of a man or woman who knows that they are imperfect even when they may appear perfect to others. Their heart is pure and their desire to know me is great. They are willing to submit themselves to me! To obey me, to admit to me that they are jacked up. To admit that they need me to heal all their broken places!

I need my daughters and sons whose hearts are not filled with pride, who don't depend on their own might and strengths to come to me. You can get everywhere with your own might yet actually be going nowhere! When I speak of the heart, I am not speaking of the vessel that blood pumps throughout. I am speaking of the being where the emotions, the love abides. The Spirit that dwells in each of you. For if the vessel is removed you have no life. However, the Spirit lives on!

In your imperfection I am perfect & in your not knowing, I am wisdom.

If my children would stop going through life acting out, what they think I want them to be and do and will go through life just being. Allowing me to dwell inside and perfect them. Then they will be free.

Listen & Obey: What is God Speaking to You

1.   When God searches your heart what does He find?

_____

_____

2.   How does pride show up in your life?

_____

_____

3/15/2021

"Let us not become weary in doing good, for at the proper time we will reap a harvest if we do not give up."

Galatians 6:9

Be not weary in doing well for the God of Abraham, Isaac, and Jacob are with you. In weary times, faint not. The God who blows winds from North, South, East, and West will be your provider. I am the God of living water. The depth of my love for you is matchless. I know the number of hairs on your head. Will the God of Abraham leave you in times of trouble? No not I saith the Lord. I will wipe away your tears. I will make a pathway for your escape.

Trust in the Lord with all your might do not lean on your own strengths but mine. I am not far. I am always near, ready, willing, and able. Lay it on the altar so that I can carry all your burdens. That which concerns you, concerns Me. In times of trouble, I am your deliverer. Find refuge in my Word. When you don't feel Me, feel Me as I am ever so present. Surrender your cares to your Father! Go in peace and I will fight your battles.

Listen & Obey: What is God Speaking to You

1.   When you are weary what is your response?

_____

_____

2.   What is standing between you and putting all your trust in the one who knows what is best for you?

_____

_____

King of Glory

"Who is the King of Glory? The Lord God strong and mighty, the Lord mighty in battle. Lift up your heads, you gates; lift them up, you ancient doors, that the King of glory may come in. Who is he, this King of Glory? The Lord Almighty, he is the king of glory."

Psalms 24: 8-10 NIV

Who is the King of Glory? The Lord God is strong and mighty!

My power is greater than any power on earth and any battle you may be facing. There is nothing impossible for the King of Glory. Rest assured that I am fully equipped to assist you with every one of your obstacles.

Give each one to Me and allow Me to be your guide. Allow Me to teach you, encourage you, and to love you. Listen with your heart for my still small voice. Listen for me in the breeze, see me through the eyes of your children. Accept my comfort. Let the glory of the Lord fill you.

Listen & Obey: What is God Speaking to You

1.   How has God showed up for you in your life? List the first three things that come to mind.

_____

_____

2.   What has God promised you?

_____

_____

3/21/21

I will rejoice in the Lord at all times. His praises shall forever be in my mouth. I shall rejoice even in the bad times, for in times of trouble, He is My refuge. In times of trouble, I can call on Him. In times of trouble, He will teach me how to trust and depend on Him. In times of trouble, I will praise him, for it confuses the enemy. I will rejoice in times of trouble.

It will be difficult to rejoice as I am fighting against my flesh, but as I continue to rejoice the Spirit of the Lord will take over and sustain me. He will strengthen me in my weakness. My God will deliver me and when I am delivered, I will come forth as pure gold. Therefore, I choose to rejoice in the Lord forever more, Rejoice.

Listen & Obey: What is God Speaking to You

1. Do you only rejoice when things in your life are going well?

_____

_____

2. What posture will you take when trouble comes your way?

_____

_____

12/19/2011

Bless the Lord, oh my soul and all that is within me bless His holy Name! I am your rock, your sword, your shield. Nothing, not death or life, shall separate you from the love of God. Everything is in the master's hand. Holy is His name, worship, and give God praise. I am in charge of all things great and small. Humble yourself to me, bow down before me in worship. Praise me your God, Great Jehovah for all things.

Continue to worship Me in spirit and in truth. I am the source of your strength, your protector. I favor you. The plans I have for you are great. Be still and know that I am the almighty one, the only one. Seek me in the good times and bad times. I'm with you, holding you, carrying you and directing you. Listen for me in the winds, rain, thunder, and lightning. I am here, do not be dismayed.

Listen & Obey: What is God Speaking to You

1.   God says that nothing will ever separate us from the Love of God. Can you say the same thing about your love for him?

_____

_____

2. How often do you take time throughout your day to commune with Him?

_____

_____

10/15/2020

Lord, I am feeling weak and vulnerable right now. Not really understanding truly why and maybe I do but don't want to confront what I'm feeling on the inside. I need your help. Fill my empty places with your love and your desires for Me. Help me to manifest these things in my life.

Release to me all your concerns. Trust that the way has already been made and the provisions already provided. I will never leave you or forsake you. God's grace is sufficient! His hands are stretched and opened wide. Fall into His arms of healing and protection. He will bring you unspeakable joy, life unexplainable! Seek ye first and all these things will be added unto thee. Praise Him as blessings flow from the Father.

Listen & Obey: What is God Speaking to You

1.   Sit in a quiet place, it could be your closet, your car, in a park wherever you can be alone. Close your eyes and ask God to fill your empty places. Write down what you felt in that moment.

_____

_____

2.   Where does your joy come from, and does it include God?

_____

_____

Vision

"Blessed are those who find wisdom, those who gain understanding, for she is more profitable than silver and yields better returns than gold. She is more precious than rubies; nothing you desire can compare with her."

Proverbs 3:13-15

What does it say about your vision when you look at yourself and only see stains? When you look in the mirror and you only see blemishes? When you look at your clothes, you only see rags. When you look at your body and you turn your head? What does it say about your vision when you try so hard to hide how you feel inside? When you need makeup to cover up the blemishes? When you speak loudly to cover up your lack of self-confidence, when you have to buy clothes to cover up your insecurities? What does it say about your vision?

What does God say about you? How does God see you? He says that you are wonderfully and beautifully made. God says that you are more than enough! He says that you are worthy! God says that you are more precious than jewels!

Listen & Obey: What is God Speaking to You

1.   What is it that you keep trying to cover up because you don't want to confront it?

_____

_____

2.   I encourage you to invite God in so that He can reveal and heal that area of your life that may hinder you from moving forward. What are ways you can begin to invite God in?

_____

_____

10/09/2015

As the night falls and sleep awaits, I pray. I pray that His love encompasses me and calms my mind & removes all my fears. Before I slumber, I spend time with my Father. The King of Kings and Lord of Lords. Not only is He my Father, but He is my Heavenly Father, He is my comforter, my friend, he's my everything! When my days seem long, and I grow weary I call upon his name so that he hears me. I long to feel his presence, his anointing, his love, his peace, and his warm embrace.

Before I slumber I long to feel his presence as he holds me in his arms. His warm embrace puts me to sleep. As I slumber, I know His will, will be done in my life. As I lay down to sleep, my prayer is that He keeps away the dark entities that often come to interrupt my rest. I not only pray that He protects me as I sleep, but that He controls my thoughts, so that I can have peaceful rest. I invite the Lord into my sleep. It's when I close my eyes at night that I want to be rejuvenated and restored. There are nights when I've fallen short of rejuvenation and restoration! Yet, I pray, and I invite Him in because I know that rest lies within Him.

Listen & Obey: What is God Speaking to You

1. Does your nightly routine include spending time with God?

_____

_____

2.How do you feel when you find yourself overwhelmed with life's troubles? What is your remedy?

_____

_____

Alone

"He heals the brokenhearted and binds up their wounds."

Psalm 147:3

What do you do when you feel so alone? The door closes and tears begin to fall. Where do you fit? Your heart tugs and longs for a love you used to know! There is nothing there, just emptiness. What am I supposed to do with this? I'm lost! I'm lonely!

He says let me heal that emptiness. Let me fill your heart with joy. Know that for every closed door, I will open several others. This pain you feel is only temporary. It's in this place you will find me. Just invite me in as I am a gentleman, I won't force you to accept me. I know you have felt me tugging at you. You've heard my whispers. There is no love greater than my love. I love you unconditionally. I want to make you whole so that you can walk in my fullness. So that when man says you are not enough, you know that you are more than enough. I can take a lonely moment and fill you with me. My everlasting love. I will encourage and teach you how to walk with me because in my presence amazing things happen. You will no longer feel empty or lonely. I want to fill you with the joy and the love of Abba!

Listen & Obey: What is God Speaking to You

1.   *What do you do when it seems like the weight of the world is on your shoulders?*

_____

_____

2.   *How do you respond to loneliness?*

_____

_____

My Provider

"He raises the poor from the dust and lifts the needy from the ash heap; he seats them with princes and has them inherit a throne of honor. 'For the foundations of the earth are the Lord's; on them he has set the world. "

1 Samuel 2:8

God is so awesome! He is so amazing! He is worthy to be praised. Lord, I love, and I adore you. Blessed be the name of my Lord and Savior Jesus Christ. God's mercy endures forever! In times of trouble, he shall hide me. Thy rod and thy staff shall comfort me. I will wait on the Lord and be of good courage for He strengthens my heart. The day shall come, and His glory will be revealed. His Angels will march as soldiers! They shall be your guards! People will marvel at the wonders of your Father! The Heavens are opening! God's blessings shall prevail.

Can't you see that I am with you? That I always keep my promises. You say how much you love me, but you can't fathom how deep my love for you flows. My love for you is immeasurable. I've seen the tears you've cried, the sacrifices you've made. My glory shall overtake you and you will walk in bountiful blessings. You will testify of my goodness and mercy for all things will be added unto thee. Continue to usher in the Holy Spirit for my spirit will guide you.

Listen & Obey: What is God Speaking to You

1. Are you willing to wait on God even when it seems that He will not show up for you?

_____

_____

2. Will you trust that His timing is always perfect?

_____

_____

What will be your response as you wait?

_____

_____

Sit at my Feet

"Cast your cares on the Lord and he will sustain you; he will never let the righteous be forsaken."

Psalm 55:22 NIV

Sit at my feet and dwell with me. Sit at my feet and worship me. Sit at my feet and simply talk to me. I am your friend. I am all that you need. Your joy, your peace, your understanding, your wisdom, your provisions are all found in me. Take the time to sit at my feet. It's in my presence that your life will be restored.

It's in my presence in the time spent with me you become more comfortable, more secure no longer doubting, your encounters with your daddy! I am waiting for you to sit at my feet. I am pleased when you sit at my feet and bring all your cares of this world to me. Even if you do not feel that I am near I need you to trust that I am there and I hear every word. Find peace in those moments as you reflect on every time you called me, and I answered. Think of every time I have shown up on your behalf even the times when you didn't think to call on me. I was there! I will never leave you or forsake you. All of your courage and confidence come in those moments because you have already sat at my feet.

Listen & Obey: What is God Speaking to You

1.   What brings you peace? Describe how it makes you feel, and does it involve God?

_____

_____

2.   Do you have peace? If not from reading this passage, think of something you can incorporate in your life daily that will help you gradually gain peace?

_____

_____

Sovereign God!

"Oh, the depth of the riches of the wisdom and knowledge of God! How unsearchable his judgements, and his paths beyond tracing out! Who has known the mind of the Lord? Or who has been his counselor? Who has ever given to God, that God should repay them? For from him and through him are all things. To him be the glory forever! Amen."

Romans 11:33-36 NIV

He's a sovereign God! He's the ruler of all things. He's a sovereign God; He hears our cries through the pain. He's a sovereign God, trust in Him and never fear. He's a sovereign God who knows that He is always near!

Though the world around us seems so very dark. The Sovereign God we serve is greater than darkness. Trust in Him and never doubt the Sovereign God He reigns throughout. Trust in God and never doubt, our sovereign God will always bring us out.

He's the sovereign God, Master of the Universe. He's my Sovereign God, my peace, my love, my joy on earth! My provider, my protector, my shield! My Sovereign God! He knows just who I am.

He's so sovereign, so majestic, so omnipotent, so incredible. My Sovereign God is irreplaceable. Get to know my Sovereign God. Allow Him to be your joy, your peace, your hope, and to consume your dreams! The Sovereign ruler, redeemer, master of all things. Worship and pray to the Sovereign God and trust that He will always make away.

Listen & Obey: What is God Speaking to You

1.   Who/What can measure up to the power of God?

_____

_____

2.   Do you trust more in the power of God or in the power of man? Does your actions line up with your words?

_____

_____

Secret Place

"But when you pray, go into your room, close the door, and pray to your father, who is unseen. Then your Father, who sees what is done in secret, will reward you."

Matthew 6:6 NIV

"You are my refuge and my shield; I have put my hope in your word."

Psalm 119:114

As I sit still in my secret place with my Father, I invite him in! I long to feel his presence. I long to feel his embrace. As I sit in my secret place I begin to pray. I begin to worship Him. I sing songs of praises, hands lifted high! His presence encompasses me! His love overwhelms me as I sit in my secret place with Him. It's in my secret place that I pour my heart out to Him. I cry out to my Father! I long to hear His voice!

In my secret place, He reveals Himself to me. His presence consumes me.

Sometimes I cry, sometimes I'm still. The peace I feel is so amazing. I feel His love for me as I sit in my secret place with Him. He reminds me of the promises He's made! He reminds me of His grace and mercy! He tells me that I am His own. He reveals the plans He has for me. He instructs me, He teaches me, He encourages me! Oh, how I love Him! It's in my secret place with Him I find strength.

Listen & Obey: What is God Speaking to You

1. Do you have a secret place where you spend time with God? If yes where? If no I encourage you to find a place where you can have alone time with God. My secret place is my closet.

_____

_____

2. What do you experience in your secret place or what would you like to experience in your secret place?

_____

_____

He loves Me

"But God demonstrates his own love for us in this: while we were still sinners, Christ died for us."

Romans 5:8 NIV

God loves me so much! He loves me more than I can love myself and more than anyone else could ever love me! He loves me so much that He gave His life for me. What a sacrifice! His life, just for me. I could never repay him for such an ultimate sacrifice. Oh, how He loves me! When I fall short, He still loves me! When I put Him on a shelf, He still loves me! When I doubt Him, He still loves me! When I sin against Him, He still loves me! When I disobey Him, He still loves me! There is nothing I can do that will stop Him from loving me! I don't deserve His love! Who can love me like that, no one but God! He loves me in spite of me! He loves me through all my imperfections. I don't deserve it. When I think about all the times I've messed up, He never stopped loving me! He never will! There is truly no love greater than Jesus!

Listen & Obey: What is God Speaking to You

1. What does God's love mean to you?

   _____

   _____

2. When was the last time you were reminded of God's love for you?

   _____

   _____

Grateful

"Enter his gates with thanksgiving and his courts with praise; give thanks to him and his praise his name. For the Lord is good and his love endures forever; his faithfulness continues through all generations."

Psalms 100:3-5

Grateful is my posture as I am reminded that God has not forgotten about me. There have been many long days and sleepless nights, but He has not forgotten about me. I am so thankful. Times when I wanted to give up , when I didn't think, I was going to make it, when I thought he had given up on me and that he ignored my tears and prayers, I am reminded that he hasn't forgotten about me. My heart is full of gratitude. I'm so full that I raise my hands high and tears flow. Tears of thankfulness. Words of exaltation to my Father in Heaven.

The testing of my faith, the heartache, hurt, rejection, and disappointment were necessary growing pains. It was in those moments God was nurturing me. He was teaching me. He was preparing me for his call His way! I am so grateful! It's with a sincere heart that I thank God. As I am reminded that He has not forgotten about me. Every promise that He has made shall come forth. I wait with anticipation for the many blessings he has in store for me.

Listen & Obey: What is God Speaking to You

1. What are you grateful for today?

   _____

   _____

2. Think of a time when your faith was tested, and you wanted to give up – what kept you going?

   _____

   _____

Do the Work!

"What good is it, my brothers, and sisters, if someone claims to have faith but has no deeds? Can such faith save them? Suppose a brother or a sister is without clothes and daily food. If one of you says to them, "Go in peace; keep warm and well fed," but does nothing about their physical needs, what good is it? In the same way, faith by itself if it is not accompanied by action, is dead."

James 2 14-17 NIV

God I am ready to do the work. You said faith without works is dead. I'm ready with your leadership and guidance to work. Whatever it takes, Lord, I am willing to do it. I've had so many seasons of disappointment, seasons of lack and heartache. Here I am Lord now confident in knowing you were there all along. Everything I went through was not in vain. It made me stronger. I learned more about your power, your strength, your presence, your never-ending love for me.

Things that would have caused me so much pain in the past or made me second guess who you are in my life, I now see them as opportunities for you to show up. Opportunities for you to reveal yourself to me. I see them as areas required to stretch me. Lord, as I go into these new seasons trying to reach new God given goals, I am ready to do the work. I'm ready to do what it takes.

He whispered to me, what if the work was done in the tears you cried? What if the work was done in the moments when you wanted to give up, but you mustered up the strength to stand? What if the work was done when you were lied on, talked about, you were deceived, and taken advantage of? What if the work was done when you prayed for others and spoke life into them when they were weak? Knowing you were dealing with your own afflictions. What if the work was done when you were kind to those whom you knew and know despise you? What if the work were done when you thought I forgot about you, you thought I'd left you to deal with all of this alone! The work was done in your remaining, while your faith was being strengthened, while your faith was being tested and tried. The work was done.

The buckets of tears you cried will be poured out over you like rivers from heaven equaling up to blessings upon blessings. You're wondering why things are happening for you so quickly. Why is help coming and you didn't ask for it? You'd already prayed for it. You sowed seeds and it's time to reap your harvest. Daughter, your work was already done.

Now it's time to walk in the season that I have prepared for you. Walk with the people I have placed in your life this season. The tears you've cried, and all that you endured was your work. When I've called you to it, know that I will equip you for it and provide you with all you need! The work was already done. Walk out your season because my child you have stood firm on the rock of life that tried to take you out. Covering you on that rock was me!

Listen & Obey: What is God Speaking to You

1. Has your faith and your works measured up?

_____

_____

2. What plans do you have to accomplish that thing that God has placed on the inside of you?

_____

_____

NOTES

NOTES

_____

_____

_____

_____

_____

_____

_____

_____

_____

_____

_____

_____

_____

_____

NOTES

_____

_____

_____

_____

_____

_____

_____

_____

_____

_____

_____

_____

_____

_____

_____

NOTES

Conclusion:

Trusting in the Father's voice is so necessary to fulfill his destiny for your life. It requires full obedience. In times of weakness and despair, in desperate times you must trust His voice. You may ask how do I know if it is Him speaking? What you hear can always be found in His Word. It will never be contrary to what His Word says. Listening to God and following his instructions may make you feel uncomfortable. You may find yourself asking questions like Lord, are you sure? Lord, I need confirmation! God how am I supposed to do this? I am not qualified or even Lord what do you mean, be still?

You may brush off what you hear or feel. Only for it to continue to bring itself back to you. You hear the same thing from others while in conversation, confirmation number 1, a song plays on the radio that stirs up something in your spirit, confirmation number 2, you hear a sermon on the same thing, confirmation number 3, and so on and so on. Yet you still question him. You must ask yourself could it possibly be that I know He speaks, but am I listening, or do I really want to listen? Am I ready to surrender? The issue often lies in our surrender.

It is in surrender that you find abundance in Christ. It's in surrender that he teaches us. It's in surrender that He gives you peace! Everything we need is in Him. Your hopes and your dreams for your life are great, but what if what He has called you to is greater! Can you trust that? Can you trust that the plans He has for you are greater than your own? Those of you that no longer dream He is here to restore your heart anew. He wants to give you a refreshing like no other!

He says in Jeremiah 29:11,

"I know the plans I have for you. They are plans to prosper you not to harm you plans to give you hope and a future."

He wants each of us to surrender ourselves to Him. Allow him to infiltrate every area of your life. Allow God's presence to fill you.

He wants to fill you with His Holy Ghost Power. I encourage you to give Him every area of your life that you have lost control in, also give Him every area of your life that you believe you have control over. The areas that you want to remain off limits. You see He knows about those areas as well. He is all-knowing!

Will you get it right every day, probably not, but each day as you spend more time with God, He will help you. As I am writing this book, God continues to reveal to me areas of my life that I haven't fully granted Him access to. He's able to reveal these areas to me because I'm learning how to release and surrender every part of me to him. I'm in constant communication with him. I want God's correction and conviction. I can't say that I've always wanted this. I've come to realize I can't grow without it.

Let's face it, we need His conviction and chastisement. This is how I/we will learn how to walk in the way of the Lord! I don't want to be a hypocritical believer who

98

passes judgement on others as if I am flawless. We all fall short of the Glory of God. Because of my relationship with Him I have been able to take a look in the mirror. Sometimes what I see isn't always Godly. That's when He reminds me of His Grace!

I hope that *He Speaks* has encouraged you to begin or start back having dialogue with Jesus. He is speaking to us daily. He wants to speak to us. I have had many encounters with my Daddy Jesus throughout my life. When I begin to doubt or feel lonely, distressed, depressed, fearful, anxious, discouraged, I am reminded of all my encounters with him. I am reminded of the very first time I heard him clearly speak to me a few months after I graduated from College. I'm reminded of when I wanted to take my life and he said, "No!" I'm reminded of when I could feel His presence and he rocked me to sleep! I'm reminded that, *"He Speaks!"*

Bio

Sonya Jones Smith, author of *He Speaks* was born in Orangeburg, SC to Al and Beverly Jones. Sonya grew up in a Christian home and was taught at an early age the importance of walking with Jesus Christ. In her late teens and early adulthood, she gradually distanced herself from church.

However, she still believed in God but didn't necessarily practice her faith. Throughout her life she can recall encounters with God but didn't know him on a personal level. She always knew he was real. It wasn't until she was desperate to have a real relationship with him that her life was forever changed.

It was during some of the darkest moments of her life that the heavenly father would reveal himself and his presence to her. He on more than one occasion literally saved her life. The greatest part about this relationship is that he is the truest friend she knows. Not only during the worst of moments but every moment of every day of her life.

Made in the USA
Columbia, SC
01 February 2022